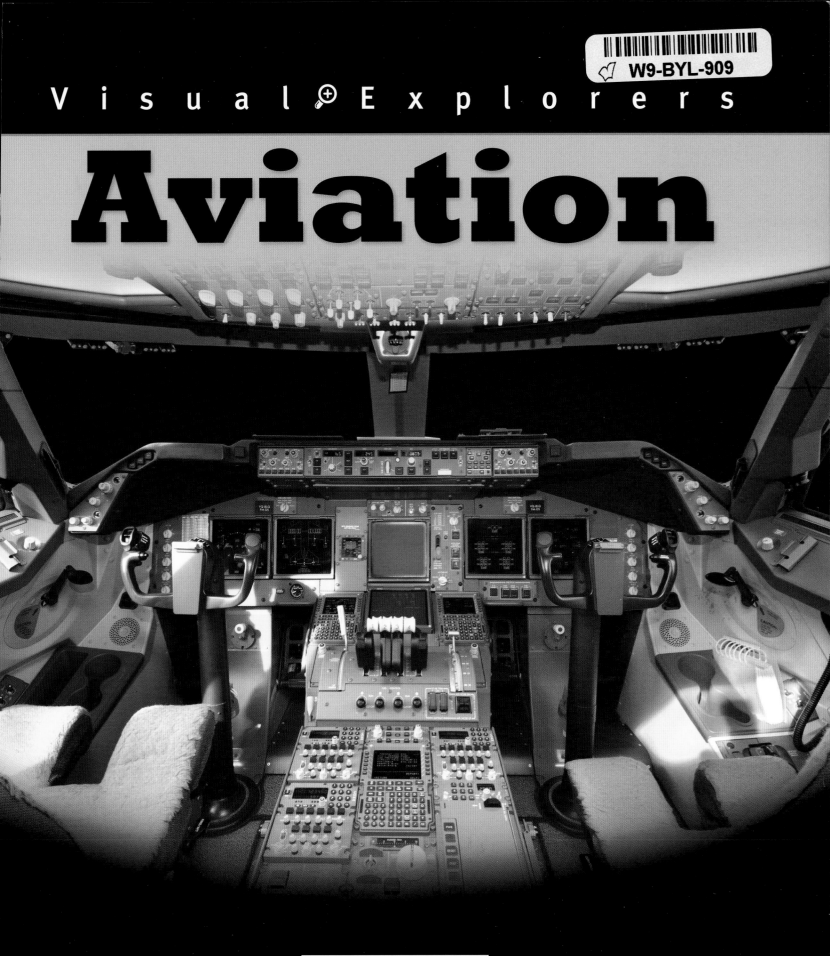

Visual ⊕ Explorers

Aviation

BARRON'S

All inquiries should be addressed to:
Barron's Educational Series, Inc.
250 Wireless Blvd.
Hauppauge, New York 11788
www.barronseduc.com

ISBN: 978-1-4380-1080-9
Library of Congress Control Number: 2017941025

Date of Manufacture: July 2017
Manufactured by: Toppan Leefung Printing Co., Ltd., Shenzhen, China

9 8 7 6 5 4 3 2 1

Photo credits:
Image credits: (t) top, (c) center, (b) bottom, (l) left, (r) right, FF (Fact file)

Aeros Company – p29 (tcr). **Airbus Industries/Airbus Helicopters** – FC (bcr) Anthony Pecchi. p23 (bl) Anthony Pecchi. p30 (bl).
Alamy – p23 (cl) US Navy Photo. p24 (main) Aurora Photos. **Boom Technology** – FC (bl). p31 (bl). **Boston Public Library, Leslie
Jones Collection,** courtesy of – p4 (br). **Flickr** – FC (br). BC (tcl). p5 (tr) Kärlis Dambräns. p10 (main) Paul Parkinson LRPS. p11 (br).
p14 (bl). p15 (c). p16 (main) Pentakrom. p19 (br). p29 (br) Jmarie999. **Hybrid Air Vehicles Ltd** – p9 (bl). **ICON Aircraft** – p21 (br).
Imaginactive – p31 (tr–br) Abhishek Roy, LunaticKoncepts, Martin Rico, Adolfo Esquivel, Jan Metelka. **Look and Learn History
Picture Library** – p5 (c) Ferdinando Tacconi (artist). **NASA**– p7 (b), p11 (bl). p18 (bl). p19 (tl), (r). **Orbis Flying Eye Hospital**– p25
(cl). **Parabatix** – p29 (bl) Louis Garnier. **Piaggio Aerospace** – p13 (b) Bruno Damascelli. **Public domain** – p6 (main), (br). p7 (t),
(c) J.Klank. p8 (cl). p9 (tl) US Navy, (cl). p10 (br) US Air Force. p11 (tl). p12 (bl), p14 (main) US Air Force/Judson Brohmer. p15 (tl),
(bl) US Air Force. p17 (cr) Aero Icarus, Dave Sizer, Steve Fitzgerald. p19 (bl) US Air Force, (br). p20 (bl) Don Boyd and US Air Force.
p21 (tl) US Navy, (cl), (bl) Oleg V. Belyakov/AirTeamImages. (tr) Tony Hisgett, (cr). p23 (tl), p25 (tr–br). p26 (bl), (main) US Air Force/
Master Sgt. Donald Allen. p27 (tl) Paul Nash (artist). p27 (cl) US Air Force/Master Sgt. Karen Tomasik, (c), (bl) US Air Force,
(tr–br). p29 (tl), (tc) Adrian Pingstone, (cl) Theresa Martinez, (tr) Anthony Applyard. p30 (main) Thames Estuary Research and
Development Company. **Royal Flying Doctor Service** – p25 (tl). **Shutterstock** – FC (main) G Tipene, (bcr) 1989studio. BC (tl) Chas
Clausen, (tcr) KarevAnton, (tr) ANURAKE SINGTO-ON. p1 Fasttailwind. p2 Anurake Singto-on. p4 (main) magicinfoto. p5 (tl)
Alexander Mazurkevich. p8 (main) jgolby. p11 (tr) Kuzmenko Viktoria photografer, (cl) Sinesp, (cr) Alexandra Lande. p12 (main)
Paul Drabot, (background) Indy Photo. p13 (c) SpaceKris. p16 (bl) kittipong kongwatmai. p17 (tl) G Tipene, (tr) jremes84, (cl)
Harvepino, (bl) Fasttailwind, (tr) Vytautas Kielaitis. p18 (main) Markus Schmal. p19 (cl) tratong, (tr) cpaulfell. p20 (main)
McCarthy's PhotoWorks. p22 (main) Nightman 1965 (helicopter) Andy Lidstone, (br) Paul Drabot. p23 (tr) Pulushkina Svetlana.
p24 (bl) Monkey Business Images. p25 (bl) Blend Images. p28 (main) Mariusz Szczygiel, (bl) James A. Harris. p29 (br) Goran
Bogicevic. p32 (br) Richard A. McGuirk. (background) kzww. **Solar Impulse** – p31 (tl). **Virgin Galactic** – p31 (cl).

Introduction

Although curiosity about flight has been in the back of humankind's mind since ancient times, only in the last 100 years have we made it possible for people to travel through the air. Since the invention of the first plane, aviation has taken incredible steps forward to become the industry we know today. From fighter jets to seaplanes, air travel is now a huge part of our everyday lives, not only transporting people and goods around the world but also helping with military operations and saving lives.

Contents

Read on to find out more about the exciting world of aviation...

What is aviation?

Aviation is the flying of aircraft and the development and **production** of machines that can fly. There are many different flying **machines**. They are either lighter-than-air craft, such as **airships** and hot air balloons, or heavier-than-air craft, like gliders, helicopters, and **spacecraft**. Aircraft transport **people** to far-flung vacation destinations and business meetings, deliver cargo around the **world**, and are vital for military operations and **civil** emergencies. Aviation is a huge worldwide industry that both brings people together and **tears** them apart through conflict.

In barely 100 years, powered aviation developed from a single-seated airplane to an 853-seat A380.

Facts and figures

Amazing aviation statistics

85: Aircraft that have vanished without a trace from 1948 to 2014.

23,600: Passenger and cargo aircraft in regular service in 2016.

39,620: New passenger and cargo aircraft needed by 2037.

50,000: Air routes in the world.

102,465: Average number of flights in one day.

1 million: Passengers in the air at any one time.

10 million: People boarding planes around the world every day.

3.5 billion: Passengers carried in 2015 by all commercial airplane services.

The world's largest passenger airplane, the 239.5-foot (73-meter)-long Airbus A380, with its 262.5-foot (80-meter) wingspan

Did you know?

Man-kites appeared in China in 588 AD, and then in Japan in the 1500s. Western interest was sparked in the 1890s, when a soldier could be lifted by a kite to do aerial observations.

Types of aviation

Civil aviation is scheduled air transport and general aviation—from business jets to hot air balloons. Military aviation is air power used in defense and war.

Airborne heroes

The FAI Gold Air Medal is aviation's highest honor. In 2002 it was won by Steve Fossett for his solo balloon orbit of the world.

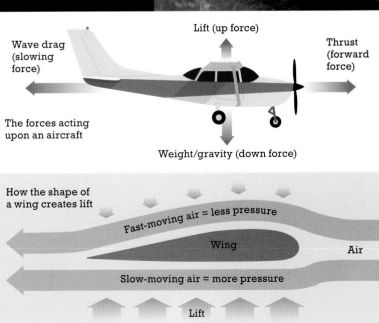
Chinese paper lanterns were the first lighter-than-air craft

Antonov An-225, the world's heaviest aircraft

Lighter or heavier

The two types of flight are lighter-than-air and heavier-than-air. Gases, like hot air and helium, are lighter than air and, when used in a balloon-like container, will lift the container off the ground. Heavier-than-air craft use aerodynamic lift with wings or rotors, and engine lift by propellers or jet engines.

Cayley's glider achieved flight 50 years before the Wright brothers

Lift (up force)

Wave drag (slowing force)

Thrust (forward force)

The forces acting upon an aircraft

Weight/gravity (down force)

How the shape of a wing creates lift

Fast-moving air = less pressure

Wing

Air

Slow-moving air = more pressure

Lift

Father of aviation

Sir George Cayley (1773–1857) was the first to understand the forces of heavier-than-air flight. These forces are weight, lift, drag, and thrust. In 1853 his workshop-built glider flew 200 yds (183 m) before crash landing—its passenger uninjured. The curved surfaces of the glider's wing gave it lift.

How planes work

Wings let an airplane leave the ground by modifying the direction and pressure of the air that passes over and under them. When pressure below the wing is greater than that above, it creates lift. The engines provide the thrust to move the craft forward against the drag forces of friction and air pressure.

History of aviation

Humanity's fascination with flight dates to prehistory—the kite was invented 2,800 years ago in **China**. A Greek myth from 60–30 BCE, describing the flight of Daedalus and his son **Icarus** on feather wings attached to their **arms**, reflects how early would-be aviators studied **birds** for inspiration. But successful flight did not come quickly. **Centuries** of invention with flapping wings, steam, pedal power, and **bizarre** mechanical devices were followed by decades of trial and error. The **dream** of flight only became real when the **Wright** brothers achieved aviation history in 1903.

Facts and figures

Some aviation firsts

1797: First parachute-assisted jump
In Paris, André-Jacques Garnerin dropped over 2,000 yards (almost 2,000 m) from a hot air balloon in a 23-ft (7-m)-diameter parachute.

1906: First European airplane flight
After the success of the Wright brothers in the US, the Brazilian, Alberto Santos-Dumont, flew a heavier-than-air machine in Paris.

1911: First official airmail service
In India, Henri Piquet flew his two-seater biplane from Allahabad to Naini to deliver 6,500 letters and cards.

1919: First non-stop transatlantic flight
This 1,864-mile (3,000 km) flight by British aviators John Alcock and Arthur Brown in a Vickers Vimy went from Newfoundland, Canada, to Clifden, Ireland.

In the Greek myth, Icarus flies too close to the Sun and falls into the sea, where he drowns

First flight

Frenchmen Joseph-Michel and Jacques-Étienne Montgolfier invented the first practical air balloon. In 1783, their silk and paper balloon flew for 10 minutes.

Genius inventions

In the 1400s, Italian artist and inventor Leonardo da Vinci drew flying machines that had flapping wings or helicopter-like rotors.

Did you know?

The first recorded aviation accident occurred in 1785. Pilâtre de Rozier and Pierre Romain were killed when their hot air balloon deflated during an attempt to cross the English Channel.

6

Wright brothers

Orville and Wilbur Wright were American inventors who were the first to build and fly a heavier-than-air plane with controlled and powered flight. The historical event took place on December 17, 1903 in North Carolina. The *Flyer* was airborne for 12 seconds, covering a distance of 40.5 yards (37 meters).

Louis Blériot

On July 25, 1909, Louis Blériot became the first person to fly across the English Channel in a heavier-than-air craft. He flew the 23.6 miles (38 km) from Calais, France, to Dover, England, in an airplane of his own design—the Blériot XI monoplane. This groundbreaking flight took 36.5 minutes.

This original 1918 Blériot XI monoplane is still flying today

The greatest aviation pioneers had many setbacks before achieving success.

Steam power

Steam-powered airplanes were developed in the 1930s. Flights were short, as craft rapidly ran out of water.

Aces and races

The first powered air race was in 1909 in France. With generous prize money, such races attracted daredevil pilots and sped up airplane development.

Amelia Earhart

Amelia Earhart was the first woman to fly solo across the Atlantic Ocean. This American had already set many women's aviation records before her 1937 round-the-world attempt. But this attempt cost Earhart and navigator Fred Noonan their lives when their airplane disappeared over the Pacific Ocean.

Amelia Earhart and the Lockheed Electra she used for her fatal circumnavigation attempt

Lighter-than-air craft

Lighter-than-air craft—**aerostats**—achieve lift through the use of **buoyant** gas. All aerostats were once called balloons, while powered **balloons** that were capable of being steered horizontally were called **dirigible** balloons. Later, free-flying dirigibles became known as **airships**, and these were used during both World Wars for observation and **bombing** missions. **Tethered** balloons—floating but tied to the ground—were used to **hinder** enemy aircraft. Today, free-flying and tethered aerostats are **used** for communication, research, advertising, and sightseeing.

Facts and figures

Some aerostat-lifting gases

Hot air
Air, which is mostly oxygen and nitrogen, expands when heated, causing an aerostat to rise. A burner is used to heat air inside a hot air balloon to get lift.

Hydrogen
Early aerostats used hydrogen—the lightest element on Earth—because it was easily available, but it burns when ignited by a flame or static electricity.

Helium
Helium has good lifting capacity but is not flammable, making it an excellent aerostat gas. However, it is rare and expensive.

Coal gas
Coal gas is a mixture of gases like methane, hydrogen, and carbon monoxide, but has only half the lifting capacity of hydrogen. Though inexpensive, the carbon monoxide part is toxic.

Did you know?

In the 1940s, during World War II, some 500 tethered balloons, called barrage balloons or blimps, floated 1,640 yards (1,500 meters) over London to defend against German dive-bombers.

Hot air balloon rallies are popular, but are not the place to break the balloon altitude record of 23,000 yards (21,027 meters)!

To give an **aerostat buoyancy,** the **lifting gas must be** lighter **than the surrounding air**.

Aerostat envelope

The envelope encases the gas-filled ballonets. It is made of man-made, high-tech fabric that can resist tears.

Gondola class

A gondola is the passenger-carrying section of an airship. It hangs below the envelope. They were once open and exposed to the elements.

The USS Akron (ZR-4) flying over New York City in 1933

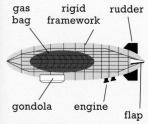
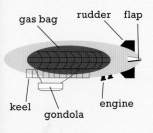
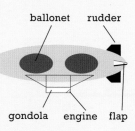
Graf Zeppelins

Rigid airships were the first type of aircraft to transport passengers and cargo over long distances. The German-made Graf Zeppelins, named for airship pioneer Count Ferdinand von Zeppelin, were powered and steerable. In 1928, their first commercial passenger flight from Germany to New York City took 111 hours.

The *Hindenburg*

The *Hindenburg* disaster in 1937, with 36 fatalities, was caused when the hydrogen-filled envelope caught fire as it moored to a landing mast. Though other airship accidents had resulted in more deaths, this disaster marked the end of the airship era.

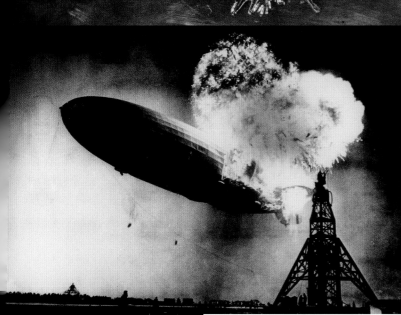

The destruction of the *Hindenburg* took less than 30 seconds

The next generation

In 2010, the Airlander 10 airship—the world's largest aircraft—was unveiled in the UK. It is a hybrid airship that uses both lighter-than-air gas and heavier-than-air aerodynamics to get lift. This giant dwarfs an A380. It is 302 feet (92 meters) long, which is eight buses end to end, and 142.7 feet (43.5 meters) wide.

Airlander 10 uses helium as its lighter-than-air gas

Gliders

Gliders are heavier-than-air craft that are **designed** to fly **without** engines. When Sir George Cayley made a glider that was **capable** of carrying a human into the air in 1853, it influenced aviation design for the next **50 years**. Even the Wright brothers practiced their flying skills in gliders. There are **three** main types of **gliders**: paragliders, hang gliders, and sailplanes. They are **mainly** used for air sports, research, spacecraft, and military warfare. Unlike **powered** craft that have four forces acting on them, gliders are subject to only **three**: lift, drag, and weight.

Wingtip smoke colors the path of an aerobatics sailplane display

Gliders ride thermals in the air just like owls and hawks.

Did you know?

The WACO CG-4 was an American troop and cargo sailplane. It was sent on one-way missions to get supplies silently into remote bases. The WACO could carry 13 people or a Jeep.

POW sailplane

The *Colditz Cock* glider was built by prisoners of war in a Colditz Castle attic in 1944, using anything at hand. The prisoners were freed, so the glider never flew.

NASA's glider

To control lunar capsule landings on Earth, NASA developed the Rogallo wing. This wing is also found on paragliders.

Otto Lilienthal

The German engineer Otto Lilienthal made over 2,000 successful glider flights. By shifting his body weight under the wing, Lilienthal controlled the glider's direction. He had a 49-foot (15-meter)-high conical hill built so that he could test his gliders in all wind conditions. He died in 1896 when his glider crashed.

Lilienthal's flapping wing glider in flight in 1895

A wingsuit turns a pilot into an aerofoil

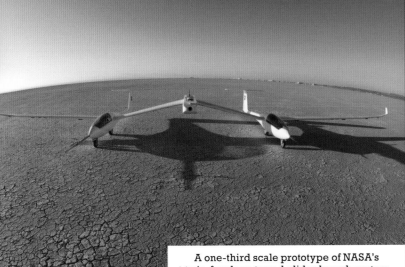

A one-third scale prototype of NASA's twin-fuselage towed glider launch system

Birdman suits

Correctly called wingsuits, this is a form of gliding in which the body's surface area is increased to achieve lift, effectively turning the human body into a wing. A parachute is used to control the landing. The first wingsuit flight, from Paris's Eiffel Tower in 1912, ended with the pilot's death.

Rocket gliders

Space shuttles can already glide into land, but NASA has been testing pilotless gliders as reusable launchers for rockets or small satellites. The glider is towed to 7.45 miles (12,000 meters) by a small plane, then a rocket motor propels the glider higher. The payload is jettisoned into low Earth orbit.

Fact file

Types of gliders

Gliders have mostly been used for recreation since the 1920s. They are less costly to own than other aircraft, and learning to fly them is relatively quick.

Paraglider
The pilot's legs are used for takeoff and landing, and he or she, seated in a suspended harness, controls the flexible wing.

Hang glider
The flexible delta wing is supported by a frame, which the pilot controls by shifting his or her body weight and moving a bar.

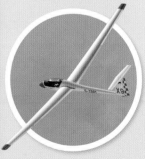

Sailplane
The pilot sits in a cockpit between long, thin, rigid wings. It has a wheeled undercarriage for a towed takeoff and for landing.

Propeller airplanes

Airplanes are **either** propeller-driven or jet-powered. A propeller, also called an **airscrew**, is a mechanical device consisting of rotating **blades** that moves craft, such as aircraft or boats, forward through a gas or fluid. The propellers are powered by an **engine**, such as a piston engine or turbine engine. The **earliest** flying machines were propeller airplanes. It was the **Wright brothers** who successfully worked out how to combine **engine-powered** propellers with wings so that their *Flyer* could move upward and **forward** at the same time.

Facts and figures

Propeller planes: speed timeline

1903:
The Wright brothers' *Flyer* flew at 30 mph (48 kph).

1909:
The Blériot Xi reached 47 mph (75 kph).

1914–1918:
Fabric-covered biplanes flew at 199 mph (320 kph).

1930s:
Macchi M.C.72, a piston-powered seaplane, hit a top speed of 441 mph (709 kph).

1955:
XF-84H *Thunderscreech* experimented with a supersonic propeller and turbine engine, but did not exceed 520 mph (837 kph).

1960:
Tupolev Tu-114 holds the propeller speed record of 541 mph (871 kph).

1989:
The F8F Bearcat *Rare Bear*, a piston-powered airplane, hit 528 mph (850 kph).

Did you know?

The 1930s Kalinin K-7, a heavyweight, experimental giant, required the power of eight six-bladed propellers to get off the ground. It was the biggest airplane built before the jet age.

Propeller planes, such as Mustangs and Spitfires, pictured here, were used throughout World War II

Wooden propellers

The first propellers were carved by hand from solid or laminated wood. Today, they also use lightweight metals and composites.

Piston engines

Traditional propeller-driven aircraft use one or more pistons to convert pressure into a rotating motion. Today, piston engines are mainly used in light aircraft.

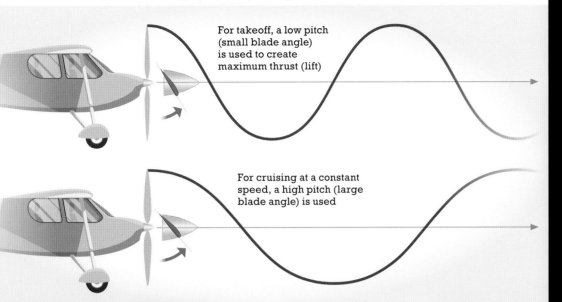

How propellers adjust the power of their thrust

For takeoff, a low pitch (small blade angle) is used to create maximum thrust (lift)

For cruising at a constant speed, a high pitch (large blade angle) is used

How they work

Propellers, like wings, are aerofoils that create a pressure difference: low pressure in front of the propeller and high pressure behind. As the blades rotate, a forward thrust is produced. The rotation is driven by a piston, turboprop, or jet engine. To adjust the power of the thrust, the angle (pitch) of the propeller blades is changed.

Counter-rotate

It is usual for all propellers on an aircraft to rotate in the same direction, but on the Airbus A400M each pair on a wing turns in opposite directions (they counter-rotate). This increases this transport airplane's lift and reduces air disturbance on the wings.

The counter-rotating, scimitar-shaped propellers on an Airbus A400M

A propeller is like a spinning wing that produces lift in a forward direction.

Blade efficiency

Propellers are not used on high-speed aircraft, as propellers lose efficiency at higher speeds.

Stunt planes

Propeller craft are best suited to aerobatic stunts such as spins, rolls, and loops, as their low speeds allow for tighter turns.

Pull or push?

Most propeller airplanes have propellers on the nose or in front of the wings to pull the craft through the air. Some are push–pull with propellers on the nose and at the tail end of the fuselage. Rear-facing propellers, positioned behind the engines, create a pusher configuration.

The rear-facing turboprop engines of the Piaggio Avanti EVO

Jet airplanes

In the years before the outbreak of **World War II**, two men raced to **invent** the first jet-powered aircraft. Their successes revolutionized the air industry. Initially, it was **military** aircraft that took advantage of the innovation, but it was not **long** before the jet **engine** transformed commercial travel. Air freight capacity increased, and the **"jet age"** made air travel an everyday form of transport. The journey from the first scheduled jet **airliner** to the turbojet-powered supersonic **Concorde** took less than two decades. Today, the majority of airplanes are powered by **jet** engines.

Facts and figures

Early jet engine development

1926: Theory
AA Griffith proposes the viability of jet engines.

1929: Invention
English engineer, Sir Frank Whittle, invents a jet engine in which an enclosed fan, driven by a gas turbine, produces fast air flow.

1936: Testing
Whittle builds a test engine, but lacks the money for development and testing.

1939: Operational
A Heinkel He 178, the first jet-engine-powered aircraft, is built by a German physicist, Hans von Ohain.

1942: The jet age
The Messerschmidt Me 262 is the first operational jet fighter.

1952: Commercial jet
The de Havilland Comet jet airliner flies its first scheduled passenger service from Britain.

Did you know?

The world's first jet-engine aircraft, the Heinkel He 178, took to the air for demonstrations just days before the start of World War II. The engine's air inlet was in the nose.

The SR71's record stood for 40 years until the X-43A flew at Mach 6.8!

The Lockheed SR71 *Blackbird* spy airplane flew at 3.2 times the speed of sound

Speed

Jet aircraft fly more efficiently at high altitudes than do propeller-powered aircraft. This makes jet aircraft better for high altitude, long-distance travel.

Sound barrier

After the jet engine, the target was to fly faster than the speed of sound, 760 mph (1,223.1 kph) or Mach 1. Charles "Chuck" Yeager succeeded in 1947 in his rocket-powered Bell X-1.

Stress fracture accidents overshadowed the de Havilland Comet's place in aviation history

Commercial jet aircraft

Passenger aircraft with two or four jet engines entered service in the 1950s, becoming the luxury way to travel. The jet airlines meant quicker travel. The flight from London, UK, to Johannesburg, South Africa, was cut by 5 hours even though it made five stops en route.

Fighters

Jet fighter planes have been designed to fight in the air against other fighter planes. To do this, jet fighters are small, fast, and easy to handle by their pilots. Their agility and precision is proven when used in aerobatics. In a US Air Force Thunderbirds' reflection pass, a pair of F-16s fly 39 inches (100 cm) apart at 450 miles (724 km) per hour.

Private jets

Private jets are privately owned, often by companies and governments, or are hired, along with the pilot and crew, for a specific journey. Air Force One is the call-sign for two specially customized jets that transport the US president.

Two Thunderbird F-16 fighter jets do a reflection pass at an air show

Air Force One has three floors and is equipped with an operating theater

Fact file

How an A380's jet engine works

A jet engine is powerful. An A380's four engines generate enough thrust to get the 631.6-ton (573,000-kg), loaded craft into the air.

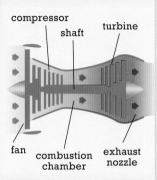

compressor
shaft
turbine
fan
combustion chamber
exhaust nozzle

Stage 1
At the front of the A380's jet engine is a fan that pulls cold air into the engine through an inlet.

Stage 2
A high-speed, bladed compressor squeezes the air, increasing its pressure eightfold, to heat it.

Stage 3
The hot compressed air is sprayed with fuel in the combustion chamber and ignited, reaching 1,652° F (900° C). The burning gases expand.

Stage 4
As the gases exit through a tapered nozzle at over 1,300 mph (2,100 kph), they turn the turbine blades, which rotate the shaft that drives the inlet fan and compressor to make a continuous cycle.

Stage 5
The gases jet back at twice the speed, pushing the airplane forward.

Passenger airliners

Airliners, or **passenger** airplanes, carry people and cargo all around the **world** for business or personal travel. The first aircraft intended to be used in this way was the **1913** Russian Sikorsky *Ilya Muromets*, but World War I led to it being **redesigned** for use as a military airplane. The 1952 British de Havilland **Comet** was to become the **first** true commercial airliner and ushered in a new era of faster, smoother air **travel**. Airliners are designed for comfort and **convenience**, and travel both nationally and internationally, often waving the flag of their home **country**.

Concorde holds the record for the fastest New York-London civil flight— 2 hours, 52 minutes, and 59 seconds!

The supersonic Concorde was retired in 2003, as it was too noisy and expensive to run

Did you know?

In the middle layer of a cabin window is a tiny hole. This regulates how much cabin pressure is exerted on the outer layer. If this layer cracks, the inner layer will remain intact.

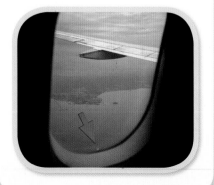

Safety first

The pre-flight safety routine draws attention to the brace-position diagrams. In an emergency, this head down, feet flat posture can save lives and prevent injuries.

Cabin pressure

Conditioned air is pumped into aircraft flying above 12,500 feet (3,800 meters). This prevents passenger sickness from a lack of oxygen.

The widest wide-body: the A380's fuselage is 23.4 ft (7.14 m) wide

The narrow-body Boeing 757's fuselage is 11.6 ft (3.54 m) wide

Body size

Commercial aircraft are classed as wide-bodied (over 16.4 ft (5 m) wide) or narrow bodied (below 16.4 ft (5 m) wide). Wide-body jets can carry up to 850 passengers on longer, popular routes. Narrow-body jets, carrying up to 300, are better suited for shorter routes. A wide-bodied cabin has two aisles and up to 11 seats per row.

The major air traffic routes over North Africa

Air traffic control

These ground-based controllers direct aircraft traffic in the sky and on the ground. They keep craft at safe distances from each other, process takeoffs and landings, and keep air traffic routes moving smoothly.

In the cockpit

In front of the pilot and first officer are instruments giving flight data on altitude, airspeed, direction, and more. The six main instruments are the altimeter, airspeed, turn/bank, vertical speed and directional indicators, and artificial horizon. Some aircraft have a heads-up display (HUD) for flight data so pilots do not have to look down into the cockpit at critical times.

The cockpit of a 747 also has a bunk and a crew bathroom

Cargo airplanes

Some aircraft are **designed** to carry goods from place to place **instead** of carrying people. These airplanes have a different structure than airliners: bigger doors, stronger **floors**, and storage space for maximum cargo, also called a **payload**. The very first goods delivered by air were rolls of silk fabric, and in the **1920s** airplanes were increasingly used to move **freight**, usually as part of a passenger service. When **cargo-only** services started in the 1940s, **larger** craft were needed, leading to the construction of oddly-named airborne **giants** like the Beluga and the Super Guppy!

In 2015, 56.4 US tons (51.2 million metric tons) of cargo were transported by air.

An Airbus super transporter model of plane is named "Beluga" after the hump-headed whale

Did you know?

The Space Carrier Aircraft (SCA) were two modified Boeing 747s. Their main job was to transport Space Shuttles from landing sites back to the Kennedy Space Center in Florida.

Record-breaker

The Antonov AN-225 *Mriya* can carry 275.6 US tons (250 m tons) of cargo, which is equal to 80 cars, and has the world's longest wingspan.

Types of cargo

The first air freight was rolls of silk in 1910. Cargo can be anything from food to machinery and even other aircraft! There are special cargo airplanes for transporting racehorses.

A Super Guppy is loaded with two T-38 supersonic jets

Fact file

Cargo airplanes

These purpose-built cargo airplanes with their open holds, strength, and weight capacity can perform many functions other than transporting freight.

Boeing C-17 Globemaster

This troop and cargo aircraft does medevacs, airlifts, and airdrops and transports the US president's limousine.

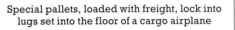

Aero Spaceline Super Guppy

The cargo area behind its hinged nose is 25 feet (7.6 meters) high and 111.5 feet (34 meters) long. NASA uses this aircraft.

Ilyushin Il-76

Used for commercial and military freight, it has also been modified for use as a simulated weightlessness trainer for astronauts.

Lockheed Martin C-130 Hercules

A transport aircraft used by the military, but also for relief aid and aerial refueling and firefighting.

Maximum space

Cargo aircraft are designed for their purpose, with the main cargo hold taking up nearly all of the space inside the fuselage. Giant doors, rear opening ramps, hinged sections, extra height and roll on–roll off systems make it possible to load cargo, large or small, quickly. Cargo airplanes have strengthened tails and extra wheels on the landing gear to cope with the heavy loads.

Plane conversion

When a plane is no longer suitable for passenger flights, it can be converted into a cargo plane. The seating is stripped out, floors are strengthened, and large doors are installed to make it suitable for cargo.

Special pallets, loaded with freight, lock into lugs set into the floor of a cargo airplane

Relief aid airdrops

Many humanitarian agencies resort to airdrops of urgent and essential supplies into conflict or disaster zones when delivery by road, rail, or boat is too dangerous or simply impossible. In Rwanda, Africa, emergency blood supplies are delivered to remote hospitals and clinics by a drone.

The parachutes are on top of emergency relief supplies ready for an airdrop

Seaplanes

Seaplanes are aircraft that can take off and land on **water**; some can also land on **solid** ground and snow. Creating a machine that could **handle** the forces of air (aerodynamics) and water (hydrodynamics) was a **challenge** for engineers in the **1910s**. By the 1940s, there were seaplane races, and luxurious **Clipper** seaplanes carried passengers around the world. Marine aviation declined as the number of **airfields** grew in the 1950s, but seaplanes still have **many** uses, like in the tourist industry or where **roads** and runways simply cannot be built.

Facts and figures

Golden age of seaplanes

1876: Patent
Alphonse Penaud patented a boat-hulled flying machine with retractable landing gear.

1898: Seaplane built
Wilhelm Kress's seaplane lacked power to take off and sank when a float collapsed.

1910: First flight
Henri Fabre's powered trimaran floatplane, the *Gnome-Omega*, was declared a success.

1914–1918: Innovation
John Porte, an aircraft designer, modified hull design so that takeoff was safer and quicker.

1919: English Channel
The first passenger flying boat service operated between Southampton, England, and Le Havre, France.

1930s: New routes
Flying boats had regular routes to all continents, except Antarctica.

The giant Global Supertanker firebomber can release 19,500 gallons (74,000 liters) of water on a blaze.

A Bombardier 415—the *Superscooper*—is an amphibious aerial firefighting aircraft

Did you know?

The Pantobase landing gear system—essentially a pair of skis—allowed a seaplane to touch down on land, water, snow, ice, or mud as long as the surface was reasonably flat.

Island hopping

For coastal, island, or remote communities inaccessible to normal aircraft, a seaplane may be the best transport option for locals, tourists, and supplies.

Useful planes

Seaplanes are used by coast guard services for air–sea rescue. Their only drawback is they cannot land or take off in large waves.

Glenn Curtiss' NC-4 seaplane was the first aircraft to cross the Atlantic Ocean

Seaplane hero

Glenn Curtiss, born in 1878 in New York, first gained recognition for his engines. One engine, fitted to a motorcycle, made him "the fastest man on Earth." His work on seaplane and amphibious craft design and his 23-day, 6-stop transatlantic flight in 1919 in a seaplane earned him the title: "Father of American Naval Aviation."

Maverick aviator

To fulfill the need for cargo airplanes, the American billionaire Howard Hughes built a wooden seaplane. Nicknamed the *Spruce Goose*, it was completed in 1947 and was one of the largest aircraft ever built. It was flown just once, and is now in a museum.

Fact file

Seaplane types

Seaplanes are a class of aircraft that includes floatplanes, flying boats, and amphibious aircraft. Below are examples from the 1930s to today.

Floatplanes
These have buoyant floats called pontoons. They are fixed to the fuselage and keep the hull off the water. The de Havilland Otter has two pontoons; other types have only one.

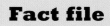

The *Spruce Goose* was 73 yards (67 m) in length with a 107-yard (98-m) wingspan

Flying boats
The fuselage provides buoyancy, and the boat-like hull is in contact with the water for takeoff and landing. This Short Empire has floats under its wings for stability.

Amphibious jet aircraft

The Russian Beriev Be-200 Altair is jet powered and can take off and land on water and land. It is a multipurpose craft that can be used for passengers and cargo, search and rescue, maritime patrols, and as an air ambulance. It is also a firefighting aircraft—its tanks can hold 3,170 gallons (12,000 liters) of water.

A Beriev Be-200 drives itself out of the water and onto land

Amphibious aircraft
This craft, like the ICON A5 or PBY Catalina, can take off and land on both water and solid ground. The special keel on a triphibian allows it to "ski" land on snow or ice.

Helicopters

Helicopters are vertical takeoff and land **(VTOL)** aircraft. They can fly forward, backward, and sideways, and **hover** unmoving in one position. To fly a helicopter, a **pilot** controls vertical (collective) movement with the **left** hand, horizontal (cyclic) movement with the right hand, and **direction** (tail rotor pedals) with both feet. Helicopters are **very** maneuverable in the air—there are even helicopter **aerobatic** teams. A helicopter can land, if conditions are good, in an **area** just larger than its rotor diameter and fuselage length, and an experienced pilot can touch down on a **slope**.

Facts and figures

Helicopter milestones

1483:
The artist and inventor Leonardo da Vinci sketched a helicopter-like device, known as the "aerial screw."

1843:
Sir George Cayley worked on a steam-powered version of da Vinci's "aerial screw."

1930:
Juan de la Cierva invented the autogyro to provide more lift.

1936:
Henrich Focke's twin-rotor helicopter was successfully tested.

1939–1941:
Igor Sikorsky's VS-300 flew in tethered and free testing.

1958:
Sikorsky built an amphibious helicopter.

2012:
There were 56,200 helicopters in service.

The Westland Sea King, used in anti-submarine warfare, is a British version of the American Sikorsky helicopter

The **word** "helicopter" derives from *helix*, meaning **spiral**, and *pteron*, for **wing**.

Did you know?

The Boeing Chinook CH-47 has two horizontal rotors, and they turn in opposite directions. These give the Chinook, a cargo and trooper carrier, greater lift, speed, and load weight.

Westland Sea King

This chopper has the most extensive war record of any aircraft, and has even survived two direct hits. Its watertight hull and pontoons mean it can land on water.

Top of the world

Helicopters and high altitudes do not go well together, but in 2005, Didier Delsalle's helicopter landed atop Mount Everest.

Igor Sikorsky

Juan de la Cierva's autogyro of the 1920s was a precursor to the helicopter, but it was the genius of Igor Sikorsky, a Russian-American aviator, who built the first working, vertical takeoff helicopter in 1939. Sikorsky modified his VS-300, and it became the world's first mass-produced helicopter.

Choppers at work

Helicopters are workhorses. They are used as passenger, cargo, and medical transport, and in land and sea search and rescue, combat, firefighting, and by the police. They can take off and land almost anywhere as long as visibility is good and can fly in rougher weather than can fixed-wing aircraft.

Igor Sikorsky on the controls of the VS-300's first tethered flight

A Sikorsky Super Stallion helicopter unloads a boat during an exercise

80% of the lift for the X^3 comes from the wing propellers

Fastest helicopter

The fastest helicopter is the Eurocopter X^3. It set its record speed of 293 mph (472 kph) in level flight in 2013. Unlike most helicopters that have a horizontal rotor and a smaller vertical rotor on the tail, the main and tail rotors on the X^3 are supplemented by two, five-bladed propellers on its wings.

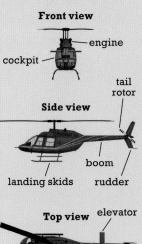

Air medical services

Fixed-wing and rotary-wing aircraft are used to transport **patients** when terrain would **defeat** road vehicles, or when a life would be jeopardized if the journey was not made in the **fastest** possible time. The first reference to an air medical service was in **France** in the **1870s** when balloons evacuated injured soldiers. Air ambulances are fitted with specialized medical equipment and **staffed** by **doctors**, paramedics, nurses—all with emergency medical training (EMT)—and a flight crew. Air ambulances **perform** miracles, from **mountain** rescues to disaster relief.

Facts and figures

All about air medical services

2–4 minutes: The time from call-out to helicopter airborne.

51.6 miles: The average distance of an air ambulance flight.

3: Number of crew on an air helicopter: pilot, doctor, and paramedic.

$3,199 (£2,500): The cost for a single UK air ambulance mission.

20 hours per week: Time volunteering in air emergency service by Britain's Prince William.

3,000: The number of medical choppers needed in China, which currently has only 20.

24/7: When air emergency services operate.

550,000 per year: The people flown in air ambulances in the US.

Did you know?

Flying an emergency medical air mission is as dangerous as combat flying because of hazards, such as frequent night flying, rough landing sites, bad weather, and more.

A doctor and patient being hoisted into an emergency air helicopter in the Swiss Alps, Europe

As lives are in the balance, air ambulances often fly where no one else will or could go.

Priority passengers

Air traffic control grants special treatment and priority handling to air ambulances when they are traveling with patients.

Air safety

To ensure safety for everyone onboard, if a member of the crew is not comfortable with a mission, it is canceled. This is known as the "three to go, one to say no" rule.

A Royal Flying Doctor Service's Pilatus PC 12/45, a single-engine turboprop

Flying doctors

The first official full-time air ambulance service was set up in 1928 in Australia. Known as the Royal Flying Doctor Service, it delivers 24-hour emergency service to those in rural and remote areas. The service has 68 aircraft, and 95% of the landings are on dirt strips less than a mile (1 km) in length.

Fact file

Air emergency transport

Rotary- and fixed-wing aircraft used as air ambulances are specially modified, equipped, and chosen to best suit the task and location.

AgustaWestland da Vinci
Designed for mountain missions, it can carry two patients (one lying down) plus a doctor and crew.

Airbus H135
Over 500 H135s are used as medical ambulances. The rear clamshell doors make access easy.

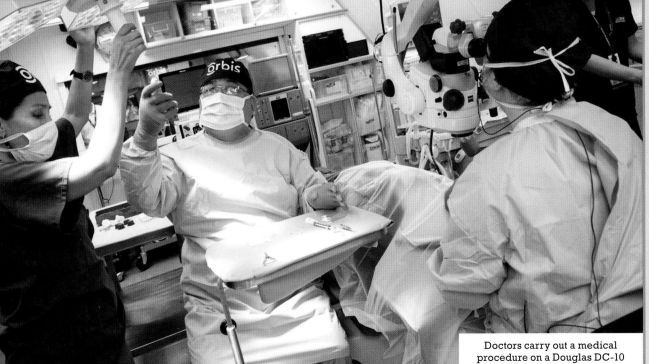

Doctors carry out a medical procedure on a Douglas DC-10

Beechcraft King Air 350
This aircraft dominates air ambulance fleets. It has speed and range and can use short, rough runways.

Hospital in the air

The Orbis Flying Eye Hospital is housed in a modified McDonnell Douglas DC-10. Its normal seating for 300 made way for medical suites, recovery room, and 46-seat classroom. Its doctors offer training in 92 countries and treatment to the world's 285 million visually-impaired people.

What's on board?

Air ambulances are supplied much like road ambulances with medication, ventilators, monitoring units, stretchers, and special supplies for very young patients. The craft's loud noise, less-than-smooth flight or confined space can prevent many medical procedures from being possible in mid-air.

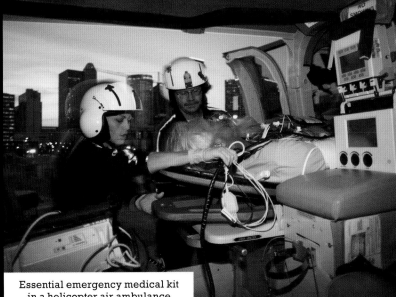

Essential emergency medical kit in a helicopter air ambulance

Gulfstream III
This is a long-distance air ambulance. It can carry up to four patients, a medical team, and four passengers.

Military airplanes

A military air force is usually a country's first line of **defense** and often the first deployed in an **attack**. Military aircraft during World War I observed **enemy** artillery, but it was not long until fighter planes and bombers were developed to **deadly** effect, with every arm of the military having an **aerial** division to some extent. Aircraft **avionics** (electronic systems), design, materials, and technology have changed warfare. **Modern** military aircraft include everything from unmanned **drones** and transport and cargo carriers to supersonic fighters and **stealth** bombers.

There are **more** than **118,000** military airplanes and **helicopters** in the **world**.

Lockheed Martin F-35 Lightning IIs are fast and agile and have advanced stealth capabilities

Did you know?

The adjustable engine nozzles on the Harrier direct thrust downward, which means it can hover, do vertical and short takeoff and landing (VTOL and STOL), and fly backward.

"Ace" status

During World War I, pilots who achieved a certain number of victories, or "kills," were known as "aces." They became public heroes and "knights of the air."

Costly machines

Developing military aircraft is an expensive business. One F-35C fighter jet will cost around $139 million.

Battles in the sky

Within 11 years of the Wright brothers' first powered flight, fighter aircraft were having close-range aerial battles (dogfights). Among the most famous air battles are the Battle of Britain (1940), Big Week (1944), MiG Alley, North Korea (1950–1951), Operation Linebacker II, North Vietnam (1972), and the Falklands War (1982).

Specific roles

Military aircraft are designed to do certain jobs. Combat aircraft include fighter and attack jets and anti-submarine and bomber aircraft. Aircraft for reconnaissance, rescue, surveillance, airborne early warning, and transport have non-combat roles.

Dogfights over the south of England during the Battle of Britain

The A-10 Thunderbolt II is a lethal combat aircraft, with 1,190.5 lbs (540 kg) of titanium

The black disk atop the non-combat E-3D Sentry is the early-warning radar

Fast and invisible

Current combat aircraft are more powerful than ever. They can fly at supersonic speeds, but ones that can fly six times the speed of sound (hypersonic) are in development. Many have low observable technology—stealth capability—so they can attack from a distance without detection by enemy radar.

F-117 Nighthawk's shape deflects radar signals, making it "invisible"

Fact file

Fighter aircraft

These four craft are examples of the world's most effective aerial combat machines. They are powerful, devastating, and technology-packed.

Panavia Tornado GR4
With a top speed of Mach 1.3, this is an all-weather attack and reconnaissance aircraft. It carries guided missiles under the wings.

Eurofighter Typhoon
This is a multi-role aircraft designed for air-to-air (dogfight) combat and air-to-surface strikes. Some 495 have been built.

Mikoyan MiG-31
Its supersonic speed—up to 1,864 mph (3,000 kph)—is used to intercept and destroy enemy bombers, drones, and cruise missiles.

Lockheed F-22 Raptor
The world's most superior fighter, it has stealth and intelligence-gathering capabilities, supersonic speed, and weaponry.

Personal aviation

The very **first** aircraft were not built for commercial or military purposes, but to satisfy a **desire** to fly. The thrill of piloting a flying **machine** has gripped the imagination of people and the brains of **inventors**, scientists, and entrepreneurs for centuries. There are many types of **craft** available beyond airplanes and helicopters. Along with well-known microlights, the **variety** of personal aviation vehicles continues to **grow** as innovators and thrill-seekers develop and test **new** ways of lifting us up into the sky. And yes, one day **everyone** will have a hoverboard!

Facts and figures

The cost of a fixed-wing plane

Purchase cost
A powered parachute about $3,200 (£2,500); a small, second-hand propeller airplane from $51,000 (£40,000) upward; and a Learjet will cost many millions.

Hidden costs
These include fuel, maintenance, storage, insurance, and crew. Runway fees vary on location and aircraft size. At Tokyo Airport, Japan, runway costs start at $5,120 (£4,000).

Sharing the costs
It is possible to part-own a plane. The co-owners are allotted flying hours and share costs.

Pilot's licence cost
Around $10,240 (£8,000) will get you a private pilot's licence in a Cessna 172. It covers training, 40 hours of flying time, written tests, exams, pilot's equipment, insurance, and even a headset!

Did you know?

The Cessna 172 Skyhawk has sold a record 43,000 units. It set a flight endurance record in 1958, traveling 150,000 miles (241,401 km) in just over 64 days without landing.

In paramotoring, a simple powered propeller is worn like a backpack

In 2013, in the US alone, there were 2.5 million flights in private aircraft.

Flying high

It is safer to fly higher. Being higher in the sky means that the pilot has more options for where to land in an emergency.

Famous flyers

Dick Rutan and Jeana Yeager flew their lightweight *Voyager* airplane non-stop around the world in 1986, without refueling. This remarkable feat was a world first.

Latest fixed-wing microlights can fly non-stop from the UK to Spain

In 1998, a flexwing microlight circumnavigated the globe

There are three types of microlights, and all are powered. Fixed-wings have the three axes of an airplane and can seat up to two people. Flexwings have a wing similar to a hang glider's, and suspended from it is a trike unit. Powered parachutes (PPCs) are parachutes with a trike suspended below the chute.

Fact file

More ways to fly

There are all sorts of aircraft that daredevils can use to fly. Some have yet to be fully realized, while others are already flight-ready.

Backpack helicopter
The motor, worn on the pilot's back, powers two sets of rotors that spin in opposite directions.

Jet packs

These devices, which are worn on the pilot's back, propel the user into the air using compressed nitrogen gas or hydrogen peroxide fuel. Often used by astronauts, they are due to become more available. Flying time is limited—around 10 minutes— and top speeds are 59.7 mph (96 kph). Hydro-jet packs use water to propel the pilot, and are relatively common.

Paramotors

Paramotors are adapted paragliders. The motor drives a propeller, which lifts the pilot airborne in a few steps. They have a top speed of 36.7 mph (59 kph), and are suited to smooth air conditions.

The Rocketbelt, a type of jet pack, can fly as high as 98 ft (30 m)

Nanolight
An ultralight powered aircraft, weighing less than 155 lbs (70 kg), is suited to thermal soaring.

Gyrocopter
Developed before the helicopter, these are still used today for sport and personal aviation.

Hopper balloon
These are single-person hot air balloons where the pilot sits in a harness instead of in a basket.

A Parabatix Sky Racer skims a paramotor just above the ground at 43.4 mph (70 kph)

The future of aviation

The most groundbreaking leap **forward** in aviation in the 20th century was in space flight, when rocket technology of the **1960s** made it possible to send people and satellites into **orbit** around the Earth and **beyond**. There are around 2,200 satellites orbiting the **planet** making communications, weather forecasting, scientific research, and more possible. But what else could the **future** hold? Engineers and scientists are **looking** for energy alternatives, **innovative** materials, cutting-edge avionics, and pilotless flying that could **transform** air travel globally and in space.

Facts and figures

Recent developments in aviation

First private spacecraft
In 2004, SpaceshipOne reached the boundary with space, 62 mi. (100 km) above Earth, and glided back safely.

Airplane taxis
Airbus Industries aims to test-fly an airborne taxi service. A network of air taxis, which take off like a helicopter but fly like a propeller airplane, will ferry a single passenger to his or her destination.

Self-healing airplanes
In 2015, a breakthrough technology that allows airplanes to repair cracks in their surfaces mid-flight was tested in a UK university.

Shape-changing wings
NASA has teamed up with US universities to research composite materials that will allow the shape of an aircraft's wing to change during flight to best suit the conditions.

Did you know?

A leading aviation company is working on a transparent plane that would give passengers a 360-degree view of their journey. Each seat would change to best suit the passenger's body shape.

A floating airport might seem far-fetched, but some airports are already built on land reclaimed from the sea

Noiseless takeoffs

Private airplanes that can take off noiselessly from a backyard will be available in the next few years. Weighing just 55 lbs (25 kg), they will be able to take off vertically.

Reusable rockets

The first rocket launchers had one-way journeys to space, but since 2015 they have returned to Earth.

95% of a flight is done on autopilot. Would you board a pilotless plane?

Energy saving

Airplanes are more fuel efficient than ever, but fossil fuel alternatives are needed. Solar power is an option that has been proven, but also possible are biomass fuels from crops, generating electricity from hydrogen, and using heat generated by the passengers to power some airplane functions.

This solar-powered airplane, *Solar Impulse 2*, circled the globe in 2016

Virgin Galactic's VSS *Unity* will carry six passengers and two pilots into space

A one-third size demonstrator of Boom Technology's XB-1

Space tourists

Only 558 people have been to space since the first manned flight in 1961, but there are several companies looking to change that. The cost of a seat on the first civilian space flights will be around $256,000 (£200,000), and space tourists will have to go through training to equip them for the rigors of a rocket launch and zero gravity.

Supersonic

The XB-1 airplane will be the fastest passenger aircraft ever made. At Mach 2.2, it will be faster than the Concorde. It is due to enter service in 2023 and carry 40 passengers from London to New York in just over 3 hours.

Fact file

Looking ahead

The developers of future air travel have to think outside the box, while taking into account the craft's purpose, power plant, and aerodynamics.

Doppelganger

This is a drone that would airlift wounded people over short distances. It could be controlled remotely or by passengers.

Mercuri

This would use 40 micro propellers in its wings to allow vertical takeoff and enable it to cover ten times the range of similar craft.

Ikaros

This is a personal glider that could drop from the edge of space, allowing the pilot to experience free-fall and zero gravity.

Subplane

This would be a military craft capable of landing in water close to shore and staying submerged until its owner returns.

Glossary

Aerodynamics
The properties or qualities of an object in terms of how air flows around it.

Aerofoil
A structure that is curved in a way to provide the most effective lift during flight—such as the shape of a wing or blade.

Aerostat
Lighter-than-air craft that achieve their lift through the use of a buoyant gas.

Altitude
A certain height in relation to sea level or ground level.

Amphibious aircraft
An aircraft that can take off and land on water as well as land.

Artillery
Armed forces that use large-scale guns and weapons.

Avionics
The electronic equipment in an aircraft.

Buoyant
Able to stay afloat (for example, in the air).

Cargo
Goods that are transported from one place to another.

Circumnavigate
Traveling around something, e.g., the world.

Civil aviation
All forms of flying that are non-military, such as scheduled flights or the use of private jets.

Commercial aviation
A part of civil aviation that involves hiring aircraft to transport people or cargo, usually for monetary gain.

Composite
Something made up of many parts or elements.

Deployed
Moving troops into action.

Dirigible
Another name for airships, which are aerostats that can be steered.

Fuselage
The main body of an aircraft.

Hull
The main body of a ship or another vessel.

Hybrid
Something made from a combination of two different things.

Hypersonic
A speed that is more than five times the speed of sound—above Mach 5.

Jettison
Remove or get rid of things from an aircraft.

Lifting gas
A gas that helps aerostats rise into the air.

Medevac
Operations where military or other casualties are evacuated by air to hospitals or safe places.

Military aviation
The use of flying machines for warfare.

Monoplane
An airplane with one pair of wings; those with two pairs are called "biplanes."

Orbit
The elliptical course of a craft around a star or planet.

Payload
Goods or material carried by a vehicle.

Pioneer
A person who is the first or among the earliest in a particular field to begin or help develop something new, and who prepares the way for others to follow suit.

Piston
A mechanical device that uses a plunging or thrusting motion.

Precursor
Something that comes before another thing of the same kind—another word for "forerunner."

Reconnaissance
The observation of an area for military purposes.

Retractable
Something that is able to be drawn back inward.

Rotor
A part of a machine that rotates—as in the blades of a helicopter.

Stealth
A design that makes its detection by radar difficult.

Stress fracture
Damage due to overuse.

Supersonic
Being able to move at a speed that is faster than the speed of sound.

Thrust
A force that propels something forward quickly and powerfully—essential for flight.

Transatlantic
Crossing over the Atlantic Ocean.

Transparent
Another word for something that is see-through.

Turbojet engine
Engines that suck air into the front, which travels through to a combustion chamber. Fuel is added and burned, creating hot gas, which is blasted out, thrusting the airplane forward.

Wave drag
A force that hinders the forward movement of an airplane because of shock waves.

Wingspan
The length of the wings on machine (or animal) from tip to tip.

Index